MW01130270

DIGGING UP THE PAST

KING TUT'S TOMB

BY EMILY ROSE OACHS

BELLWETHER MEDIA • MINNEAPOLIS, MN

TM

Are you ready to take it to the extreme? Torque books thrust you into the action-packed world of sports, vehicles, mystery, and adventure. These books may include dirt, smoke, fire, and chilling tales. **WARNING**: read at your own risk.

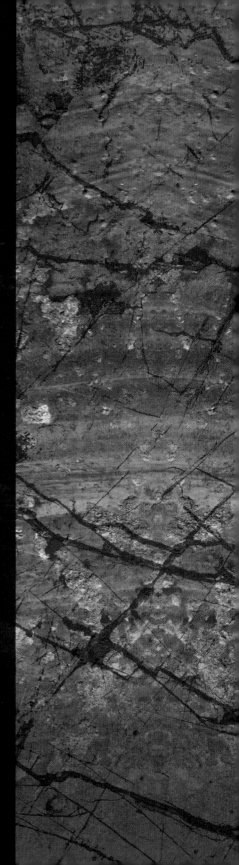

This edition first published in 2020 by Bellwether Media, Inc.

No part of this publication may be reproduced in whole or in part without written permission of the publisher. For information regarding permission, write to Bellwether Media, Inc., Attention: Permissions Department, 6012 Blue Circle Drive, Minnetonka, MN 55343.

Library of Congress Cataloging-in-Publication Data

Names: Oachs, Emily Rose, author.
Title: King Tut's Tomb / by Emily Rose Oachs.
Description: Minneapolis, MN : Bellwether Media, Inc., 2020. |
    Series: Torque: Digging Up the Past
Identifiers: LCCN 2018061014 (print) | LCCN 2019001155 (ebook) |
    ISBN 9781618916396 (ebook) | ISBN 9781644870679
    (hardcover : alk. paper)
Subjects: LCSH: Tutankhamen, King of Egypt–Tomb–Juvenile literature. |
    Egypt–Antiquities–Juvenile literature.
Classification: LCC DT87.5 (ebook) | LCC DT87.5 .O23 2020 (print) |
    DDC 932/.014092–dc23
LC record available at https://lccn.loc.gov/2018061014

Text copyright © 2020 by Bellwether Media, Inc. TORQUE and associated logos are trademarks and/or registered trademarks of Bellwether Media, Inc. SCHOLASTIC, CHILDREN'S PRESS, and associated logos are trademarks and/or registered trademarks of Scholastic Inc., 557 Broadway, New York, NY 10012.

Editor: Betsy Rathburn   Designer: Brittany McIntosh

Printed in the United States of America, North Mankato, MN.

TABLE OF CONTENTS

AN ANCIENT BURIAL PLACE

The sun beats down as you walk through a dusty desert valley. Stone steps lead you to an empty underground room. What was it like when it was filled with **ancient** treasures?

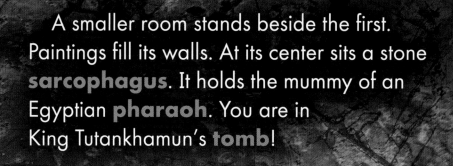

A smaller room stands beside the first. Paintings fill its walls. At its center sits a stone **sarcophagus**. It holds the mummy of an Egyptian **pharaoh**. You are in King Tutankhamun's **tomb**!

sarcophagus

THE PHARAOH'S NICKNAME

Today, King Tutankhamun is often called King Tut.

WHAT IS
KING TUT'S TOMB?

King Tut's tomb is an ancient burial place.
King Tut was buried there in 1323 BCE.
The tomb is hidden away near Luxor, Egypt.
It is more than 3,000 years old!

The tomb is famous for the riches it held. It is the most complete royal Egyptian tomb ever found!

THE BOY KING

King Tut became pharaoh when he was just nine years old. Many called him the Boy King!

WHERE IS KING TUT'S TOMB?

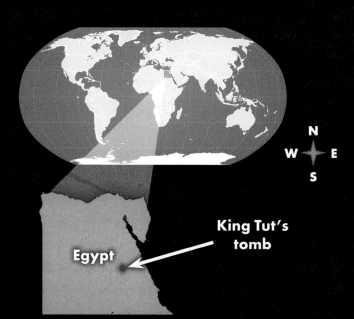

N
W E
S

Egypt

King Tut's tomb

Tutankhamun's tomb was carved deep into the **Valley of the Kings**. Its location was kept secret to try to protect it from thieves.

VALLEY OF THE KINGS
More than 60 people were buried in the Valley of the Kings!

Valley of the Kings

Officials packed the tomb with treasures, food, and clothing. At the time, Egyptians believed the souls of the dead lived forever. They thought everything in Tutankhamun's tomb would help him in the **afterlife**.

Thieves broke into Tut's tomb a few years after his burial. The thieves were caught before they could steal many treasures. They were the last people to enter the tomb for more than 3,000 years.

Within a few hundred years, King Tut's tomb was lost. Workers built huts over its entrance. The young king's burial place was forgotten.

KING TUT'S TOMB TIMELINE

1342 BCE:
Tutankhamun is born

1323 BCE:
King Tutankhamun dies and is buried in the Valley of the Kings

1333 BCE:
Tutankhamun becomes pharaoh

1914 CE:
Howard Carter begins
a search for King Tut's tomb

1923:
King Tutankhamun's
burial chamber
is opened

1922:
Carter and his team
unearth the tomb

AT LONG LAST

Howard
Carter

British **archaeologist** Howard Carter
wanted to find King Tut's tomb. He spent years
looking for it in the Valley of the Kings.

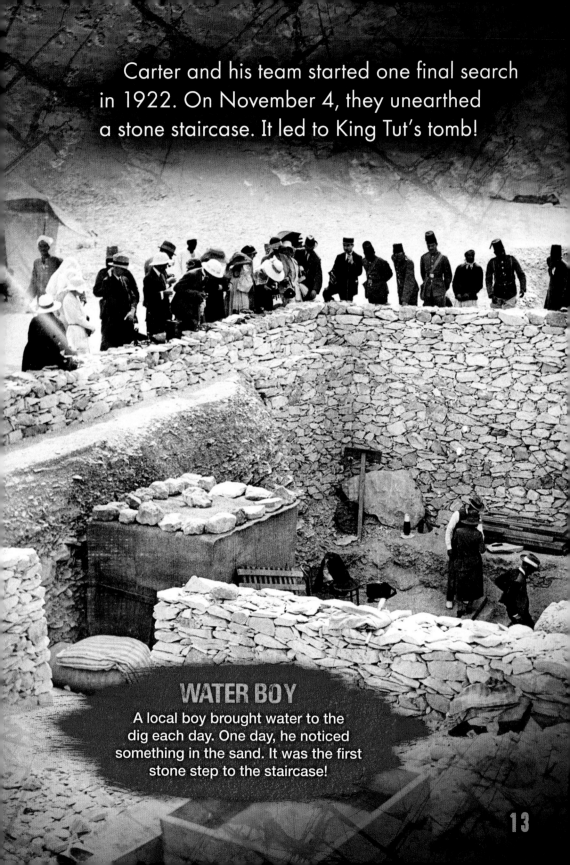

Carter and his team started one final search in 1922. On November 4, they unearthed a stone staircase. It led to King Tut's tomb!

WATER BOY

A local boy brought water to the dig each day. One day, he noticed something in the sand. It was the first stone step to the staircase!

King Tut's tomb had four small rooms. Sealed inside were 5,000 **artifacts**. Many were made of gold, ivory, and other valuable materials.

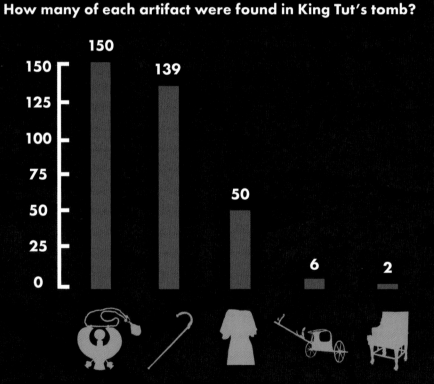

PREPARING FOR THE AFTERLIFE

How many of each artifact were found in King Tut's tomb?

jewelry items	150
walking sticks	139
pieces of clothing	50
chariots	6
thrones	2

artifacts from the tomb

The Antechamber and Annex were opened first. Weapons, **chariots**, and furniture filled the rooms. Painted chests held clothing and detailed jewelry. Statues of Tut and gods stood watch over the tomb.

15

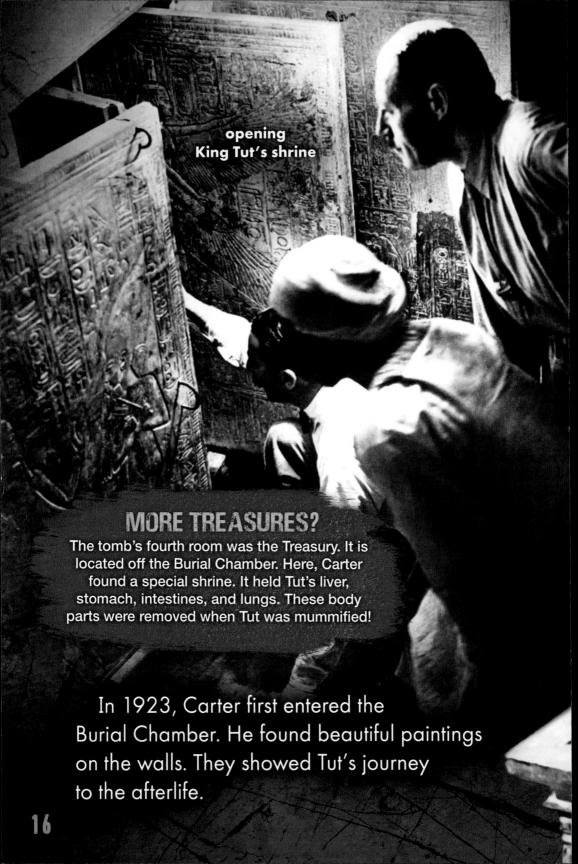

opening
King Tut's shrine

MORE TREASURES?

The tomb's fourth room was the Treasury. It is located off the Burial Chamber. Here, Carter found a special shrine. It held Tut's liver, stomach, intestines, and lungs. These body parts were removed when Tut was mummified!

In 1923, Carter first entered the Burial Chamber. He found beautiful paintings on the walls. They showed Tut's journey to the afterlife.

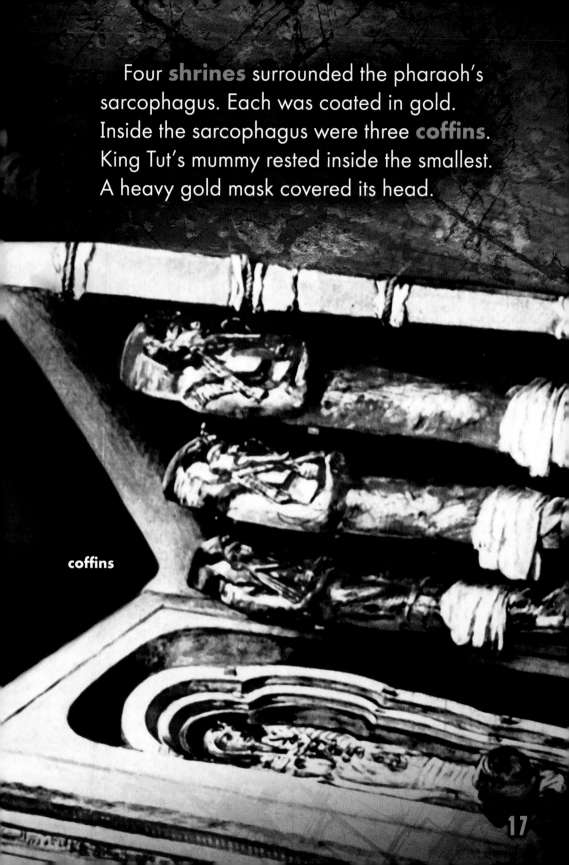

Four **shrines** surrounded the pharaoh's sarcophagus. Each was coated in gold. Inside the sarcophagus were three **coffins**. King Tut's mummy rested inside the smallest. A heavy gold mask covered its head.

coffins

PROTECTING TUT

tourists visiting
the replica tomb

Today, most artifacts are at museums.
But **tourists** can visit Tut's tomb. The Burial
Chamber still holds the mummy and sarcophagus.
But scientists worry about the damage
tourists cause.

In 2014, a **replica** of the tomb opened nearby. Now tourists can experience the tomb without harming it further!

Another large **conservation** project ended in 2018. Experts spent years cleaning and protecting the tomb and its paintings.

NO MORE ROOMS

Discovery: King Tut's tomb has no hidden rooms
Date of Discovery: 2018
Process:
1. Radar scan in 2015 showed the tomb might have hidden doorways
2. Radar scan in 2016 did not show hidden doorways
3. Radar scan in 2018 broke the tie, proving no more rooms in Tut's tomb

What It Means:
- All of Tut's treasures have been found
- Researchers must study other treasures to make more discoveries about King Tut's tomb

The Grand Egyptian Museum opened near Giza in 2019. There, visitors can see thousands of items from the tomb. Egypt is proud of King Tut. It wants to keep the pharaoh's treasures safe to share with the world!

GLOSSARY

afterlife—the place some people believe exists after death

ancient—very old

archaeologist—a scientist who studies the remains of past human life and activities

artifacts—objects that save the history and culture of a past event or place

chariots—vehicles pulled by horses

coffins—boxes that hold the bodies of the dead

conservation—the work done to protect something

pharaoh—an ancient Egyptian ruler

replica—an exact copy

sarcophagus—a coffin made out of stone

shrines—places used to store or display important or valuable objects

tomb—a building where a person is placed after death

tourists—people who travel to visit another place

Valley of the Kings—an area in Egypt where there are more than 60 tombs for ancient Egyptian royals

TO LEARN MORE

AT THE LIBRARY

Alkire, Jessie. *Investigating Tombs & Mummies*. Minneapolis, Minn.: Abdo Pub., 2019.

Farndon, John. *How to Live Like an Egyptian Mummy Maker*. Minneapolis, Minn.: Hungry Tomato, 2016.

Owen, Ruth. *King Tut: The Hidden Tomb*. New York, N.Y.: Bearport Publishing, 2017.

ON THE WEB

Factsurfer.com gives you a safe, fun way to find more information.

1. Go to www.factsurfer.com.

2. Enter "King Tut's tomb" into the search box and click 🔍.

3. Select your book cover to see a list of related web sites.

INDEX